AFTERWHILES

By the Same Author

THE OLD SWIMMIN'-HOLE
        AND 'LEVEN MORE POEMS

THE BOSS GIRL AND
        OTHER SKETCHES AND POEMS

———

BOWEN-MERRILL CO.

AFTERWHILES

BY

JAMES WHITCOMB RILEY

NINTH THOUSAND

Indianapolis
BOWEN-MERRILL CO., PUBLISHERS
1890

COPYRIGHT 1887
BY
JAMES WHITCOMB RILEY

TO HUMBOLDT RILEY

I can not say, and I will not say
That he is dead.—He is just away.

CONTENTS.

SONNETS.

IN DIALECT.

NOTE.—Acknowledgments are due the courtesy of the CENTURY MAGAZINE for reprint here of the poems " *When She Comes Home*,' and "*Nothin' to Say*."

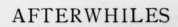

AFTERWHILES

*W*HERE are they — the Afterwhiles —
    Luring us the lengthening miles
Of our lives? Where is the dawn
With the dew across the lawn
Stroked with eager feet the far
Way the hills and valleys are?
Where the sun that smites the frown
Of the eastward-gazer down?
Where the rifted wreathes of mist
O'er us, tinged with amethyst,
Round the mountain's steep defiles?
Where are all the afterwhiles?

Afterwhile — and we will go
Thither, yon, and to and fro —
From the stifling city-streets
To the country's cool retreats —
From the riot to the rest
Where hearts beat the placidest;
Afterwhile, and we will fall
Under breezy trees, and loll
In the shade, with thirsty sight
Drinking deep the blue delight
Of the skies that will beguile
Us as children — afterwhile.

Afterwhile — and one intends
To be gentler to his friends —
To walk with them, in the hush
Of still evenings, o'er the plush
Of home-leading fields, and stand
Long at parting, hand in hand:
One, in time, will joy to take
New resolves for someone's sake,
And wear then the look that lies
Clear and pure in other eyes —
He will soothe and reconcile
His own conscience — afterwhile.

Afterwhile — we have in view
A far scene to journey to,—
Where the old home is, and where
The old mother waits us there,
Peering, as the time grows late,
Down the old path to the gate.—
How we'll click the latch that locks
In the pinks and hollyhocks,
And leap up the path once more
Where she waits us at the door! —
How we'll greet the dear old smile,
And the warm tears — afterwhile!

Ah, the endless afterwhiles! —
Leagues on leagues, and miles on miles,
In the distance far withdrawn,
Stretching on, and on, and on,
Till the fancy is footsore
And faints in the dust before
The last milestone's granite face,
Hacked with: Here Beginneth Space.
O far glimmering worlds and wings,
Mystic smiles and beckonings,
Lead us, through the shadowy aisles
Out into the afterwhiles.

HERR WEISER.

HERR WEISER! — Three-score-years-and-ten, —
  A hale white rose of his countrymen,
Transplanted here in the Hoosier loam,
And blossomy as his German home —
As blossomy, and as pure and sweet
As the cool green glen of his calm retreat,
Far withdrawn from the noisy town
Where trade goes clamoring up and down,
Whose fret and fever, and stress and strife
May not trouble his tranquil life!

Breath of rest, what a balmy gust! —
Quit of the city's heat and dust,
Jostling down by the winding road,
Through the orchard ways of his quaint abode. —
Tether the horse, as we onward fare
Under the pear-trees trailing there,
And thumping the wooden bridge at night
With lumps of ripeness and lush delight,
Till the stream, as it maunders on till dawn,
Is powdered and pelted and smiled upon.

Herr Weiser, with his wholesome face,
And the gentle blue of his eyes, and grace
Of unassuming honesty,
Be there to welcome you and me!
And what though the toil of the farm be stopped
And the tireless plans of the place be dropped,
While the prayerful master's knees are set
In beds of pansy, and mignonette,
And lily and aster and columbine,
Offered in love, as yours and mine? —

What, but a blessing of kindly thought,
Sweet as the breath of forget-me-not! —
What, but a spirit of lustrous love
White as the aster he bends above! —
What, but an odorous memory
Of the dear old man, made known to me
In days demanding a help like his,—
As sweet as the life of the lily is —
As sweet as the soul of a babe, bloom-wise
Born of a lily in paradise.

THE BEAUTIFUL CITY.

THE BEAUTIFUL CITY! Forever
    Its rapturous praises resound;
We fain would behold it—but never
    A glimpse of its glory is found:
We slacken our lips at the tender
    White breasts of our mothers to hear
Of its marvelous beauty and splendor;—
    We see—but the gleam of a tear!

Yet never the story may tire us—
    First graven in symbols of stone—
Rewritten on scrolls of papyrus,
    And parchment, and scattered and blown
By the winds of the tongues of all nations,
    Like a litter of leaves wildly whirled
Down the rack of a hundred translations,
    From the earliest lisp of the world.

7

We compass the earth and the ocean,
　From the Orient's uttermost light,
To where the last ripple in motion
　Lips hem of the skirt of the night,—
But The Beautiful City evades us—
　No spire of it glints in the sun—
No glad-bannered battlement shades us
　When all our long journey is done.

Where lies it? We question and listen;
　We lean from the mountain, or mast,
And see but dull earth, or the glisten
　Of seas inconceivably vast:
The dust of the one blurs our vision—
　The glare of the other our brain,
Nor city nor island elysian
　In all of the land or the main!

We kneel in dim fanes where the thunders
　Of organs tumultuous roll,
And the longing heart listens and wonders,
　And the eyes look aloft from the soul,

But the chanson grows fainter and fainter,
  Swoons wholly away and is dead;
And our eyes only reach where the painter
  Has dabbled a saint overhead.

The Beautiful City! O mortal,
  Fare hopefully on in thy quest,
Pass down through the green grassy portal
  That leads to the Valley of Rest,
There first passed the One who, in pity
  Of all thy great yearning, awaits
To point out The Beautiful City,
  And loosen the trump at the gates.

LOCKERBIE STREET.

SUCH a dear little street it is, nestled away
   From the noise of the city and heat of the day,
In cool shady coverts of whispering trees,
With their leaves lifted up to shake hands with the
     breeze
Which in all its wide wanderings never may meet
With a resting-place fairer than Lockerbie street!

There is such a relief, from the clangor and din
Of the heart of the town, to go loitering in
Through the dim, narrow walks, with the sheltering
     shade
Of the trees waving over the long promenade,
And littering lightly the ways of our feet
With the gold of the sunshine of Lockerbie street.

And the nights that come down the dark pathways
     of dusk,
With the stars in their tresses, and odors of musk

In their moon-woven raiments, bespangled with dews,
And looped up with lilies for lovers to use
In the songs that they sing to the tinkle and beat
Of their sweet serenadings through Lockerbie street.

O, my Lockerbie street! You are fair to be seen —
Be it noon of the day, or the rare and serene
Afternoon of the night — you are one to my heart,
And I love you above all the phrases of art,
For no language could frame, and no lips could
          repeat
My rhyme-haunted raptures of Lockerbie street.

DAS KRIST KINDEL.

I HAD fed the fire and stirred it, till the sparkles
     in delight
Snapped their saucy little fingers at the chill Decem-
     ber night;
And in dressing-gown and slippers, I had tilted back
     "my throne"—
The old split-bottomed rocker—and was musing all
     alone.

I could hear the hungry Winter prowling round the
     outer door,
And the tread of muffled footsteps on the white
     piazza floor;
But the sounds came to me only as the murmur of a
     stream
That mingled with the current of a lazy-flowing
     dream.

Like a fragrant incense rising, curled the smoke of
    my cigar,
With the lamp-light gleaming through it like a mist-
    enfolded star ; —
And as I gazed, the vapor like a curtain rolled away,
With a sound of bells that tinkled, and the clatter
    of a sleigh.

And in a vision, painted like a picture in the air,
I saw the elfish figure of a man with frosty hair —
A quaint old man that chuckled with a laugh as he
    appeared,
And with ruddy cheeks like embers in the ashes of
    his beard.

He poised himself grotesquely, in an attitude of
    mirth,
On a damask-covered hassock that was sitting on the
    hearth ;
And at a magic signal of his stubby little thumb,
I saw the fireplace changing to a bright proscenium.

And looking there, I marveled as I saw a mimic
stage
Alive with little actors of a very tender age;
And some so very tiny that they tottered as they
walked,
And lisped and purled and gurgled like the brook-
lets, when they talked.

And their faces were like lilies, and their eyes like
purest dew,
And their tresses like the shadows that the shine is
woven through;
And they each had little burdens, and a little tale to
tell
Of fairy lore, and giants, and delights delectable.

And they mixed and intermingled, weaving melody
with joy,
Till the magic circle clustered round a blooming
baby-boy;
And they threw aside their treasures in an ecstasy of
glee,
And bent, with dazzled faces, and with parted lips,
to see.

14

'Twas a wondrous little fellow, with a dainty double
    chin,
And chubby cheeks, and dimples for the smiles to
    blossom in ;
And he looked as ripe and rosy, on his bed of straw
    and reeds,
As a mellow little pippin that had tumbled in the
    weeds.

And I saw the happy mother, and a group surround-
    ing her,
That knelt with costly presents of frankincense and
    myrrh ;
And I thrilled with awe and wonder, as a murmur
    on the air
Came drifting o'er the hearing in a melody of
    prayer : —

*By the splendor in the heavens, and the hush upon the
    sea,*
And the majesty of silence reigning over Galilee,—
*We feel Thy kingly presence, and we humbly bow the
    knee*
And lift our hearts and voices in gratefulness to Thee.

Thy messenger has spoken, and our doubts have fled and
    gone
As the dark and spectral shadows of the night before
    the dawn;
And, in the kindly shelter of the light around us drawn,
We would nestle down forever in the breast we lean upon.

You have given us a shepherd — You have given us a
    guide,
And the light of Heaven grew dimmer when You sent
    Him from Your side,—
But He comes to lead Thy children where the gates
    will open wide
To welcome His returning when His works are glorified.

By the splendor in the Heavens, and the hush upon the
    sea,
And the majesty of silence reigning over Galilee,—
We feel Thy kingly presence, and we humbly bow the
    knee
And lift our hearts and voices in gratefulness to Thee.

Then the vision, slowly failing, with the words of
the refrain,
Fell swooning in the moonlight through the frosty
window-pane;
And I heard the clock proclaiming, like an eager
sentinel
Who brings the world good tidings, — "It is Christmas — all is well!"

ANSELMO.

YEARS did I vainly seek the good Lord's grace,—
   Prayed, fasted and did penance dire and dread;
Did kneel with bleeding knees and rainy face,
   And mouth the dust, with ashes on my head;
Yea, still, with knotted scourge the flesh I flayed,
   Rent fresh the wounds, and moaned and shrieked
      insanely;
And froth oozed with the pleadings that I made,
   And yet I prayed on vainly, vainly, vainly!

A time, from out of swoon, I lifted eye,
   To find a wretched outcast, gray and grim,
Bathing my brow, with many a pitying sigh,
   And I did pray God's grace might rest on him.—
Then, lo! a gentle voice fell on mine ears—
   "Thou shalt not sob in suppliance hereafter;
Take up thy prayers and wring them dry of tears,
   And lift them, white and pure, with love and
      laughter!"

      So is it now for all men else I pray;
      So is it I am blest and glad alway.

A HOME-MADE FAIRY TALE.

BUD, come here to your Uncle a spell,
  And I'll tell you something you mustn't tell —
For it's a secret and shore-nuff true,
And maybe I oughtn't to tell it to you! —
But out in the garden, under the shade
Of the apple-trees, where we romped and played
Till the moon was up, and you thought I'd gone
Fast asleep, — That was all put on!
For I was a-watchin' something queer
Goin' on there in the grass, my dear! —
'Way down deep in it, there I see
A little dude fairy who winked at me,
And snapped his fingers, and laughed as low
And fine as the whine of a mus-kee-to!
I kept still — watchin' him closer — and
I noticed a little guitar in his hand,
Which he leant 'ginst a little dead bee — and laid
His cigarette down on a clean grass-blade;

And then climbed up on the shell of a snail —
Carefully dusting his swallowtail —
And pulling up, by a waxed web-thread,
This little guitar, you remember, I said!
And there he trinkled and trilled a tune —
" My Love, so fair, Tans in the Moon!"
Till, presently, out of the clover-top
He seemed to be singing to, came, k'pop!
The purtiest, daintiest fairy face
In all this world, or any place!
Then the little ser'nader waved his hand,
As much as to say, " We'll excuse *you!* " and
I heard, as I squinted my eyelids to,
A kiss like the drip of a drop of dew!

THE SOUTH WIND AND THE SUN.

O THE South Wind and the Sun!
 How each loved the other one—
Full of fancy—full of folly—
 Full of jollity and fun!
 How they romped and ran about,
 Like two boys when school is out,
With glowing face, and lisping lip,
 Low laugh, and lifted shout!

 And the South Wind—he was dressed
 With a ribbon round his breast
That floated, flapped and fluttered
 In a riotous unrest,
 And a drapery of mist,
 From the shoulder and the wrist
Flowing backward with the motion
 Of the waving hand he kissed.

21

And the Sun had on a crown
  Wrought of gilded thistledown,
And a scarf of velvet vapor,
  And a raveled-rainbow gown;
  And his tinsel-tangled hair,
  Tossed and lost upon the air,
Was glossier and flossier
  Than any anywhere.

And the South Wind's eyes were two
  Little dancing drops of dew,
As he puffed his cheeks, and pursed his lips,
  And blew and blew and blew!
  And the Sun's — like diamond-stone,
  Brighter yet than ever known,
As he knit his brows and held his breath,
  And shone and shone and shone!

And this pair of merry fays
  Wandered through the summer days;
Arm-in-arm they went together
  Over heights of morning haze —

Over slanting slopes of lawn
They went on and on and on,
Where the daisies looked like star-tracks
Trailing up and down the dawn.

And where'er they found the top
Of a wheat-stalk droop and lop
They chucked it underneath the chin
And praised the lavish crop,
Till it lifted with the pride
Of the heads it grew beside,
And then the South Wind and the Sun
Went onward satisfied.

Over meadow-lands they tripped,
Where the dandelions dipped
In crimson foam of clover-bloom,
And dripped and dripped and dripped;
And they clinched the bumble-stings,
Gauming honey on their wings,
And bundling them in lily-bells,
With maudlin murmurings.

And the humming-bird, that hung
  Like a jewel up among
The tilted honeysuckle-horns,
  They mesmerized, and swung
  In the palpitating air,
  Drowsed with odors strange and rare,
And, with whispered laughter, slipped away,
  And left him hanging there.

And they braided blades of grass
  Where the truant had to pass;
And they wriggled through the rushes
  And the reeds of the morass,
  Where they danced, in rapture sweet,
  O'er the leaves that laid a street
Of undulant mosaic for
  The touches of their feet.

By the brook with mossy brink,
  Where the cattle came to drink,
They trilled and piped and whistled
  With the thrush and bobolink,

Till the kine, in listless pause,
  Switched their tails in mute applause,
With lifted heads, and dreamy eyes,
  And bubble-dripping jaws.

And where the melons grew,
  Streaked with yellow, green and blue,
These jolly sprites went wandering
  Through spangled paths of dew;
  And the melons, here and there,
  They made love to, everywhere,
Turning their pink souls to crimson
  With caresses fond and fair.

Over orchard walls they went,
  Where the fruited boughs were bent
Till they brushed the sward beneath them
  Where the shine and shadow blent;
  And the great green pear they shook
  Till the sallow hue forsook
Its features, and the gleam of gold
  Laughed out in every look.

And they stroked the downy cheek
  Of the peach, and smoothed it sleek,
And flushed it into splendor;
  And, with many an elfish freak,
  Gave the russet's rust a wipe—
  Prankt the rambo with a stripe,
And the winesap blushed its reddest
  As they spanked the pippins ripe.

Through the woven ambuscade
  That the twining vines had made,
They found the grapes, in clusters,
  Drinking up the shine and shade—
  Plumpt, like tiny skins of wine,
  With a vintage so divine
That the tongue of fancy tingled
  With the tang of muscadine.

And the golden-banded bees,
  Droning o'er the flowery leas,
They bridled, reined, and rode away
  Across the fragrant breeze,

Till in hollow oak and elm
  They had groomed and stabled them
In waxen stalls that oozed with dews
  Of rose and lily-stem.

Where the dusty highway leads,
  High above the wayside weeds,
They sowed the air with butterflies
  Like blooming flower-seeds,
  Till the dull grasshopper sprung
  Half a man's height up, and hung
Tranced in the heat, with whirring wings,
  And sung and sung and sung!

And they loitered, hand in hand,
  Where the snipe along the sand
Of the river ran to meet them
  As the ripple meets the land,
  Till the dragonfly, in light
  Gauzy armor, burnished bright,
Came tilting down the waters
  In a wild, bewildered flight.

And they heard the killdee's call,
And afar, the waterfall,
But the rustle of a falling leaf
They heard above it all;
And the trailing willow crept
Deeper in the tide that swept
The leafy shallop to the shore,
And wept and wept and wept!

And the fairy vessel veered
From its moorings — tacked and steered
For the center of the current —
Sailed away and disappeared:
And the burthen that it bore
From the long-enchanted shore —
"Alas! the South Wind and the Sun!"
I murmur evermore.

For the South Wind and the Sun,
Each so loves the other one,
For all his jolly folly,
And frivolity and fun,

That our love for them they weigh
  As their fickle fancies may,
And when at last we love them most,
  They laugh and sail away.

THE LOST KISS.

I PUT by the half-written poem,
   While the pen, idly trailed in my hand,
Writes on,—"Had I words to complete it,
   Who'd read it, or who'd understand?"
But the little bare feet on the stairway,
   And the faint, smothered laugh in the hall,
And the eerie-low lisp on the silence,
   Cry up to me over it all.

So I gather it up—where was broken
   The tear-faded thread of my theme,
Telling how, as one night I sat writing,
   A fairy broke in on my dream,
A little inquisitive fairy—
   My own little girl, with the gold
Of the sun in her hair, and the dewy
   Blue eyes of the fairies of old.

'Twas the dear little girl that I scolded —
  "For was it a moment like this,"
I said, "when she knew I was busy,
  To come romping in for a kiss?—
Come rowdying up from her mother,
  And clamoring there at my knee
For 'One 'ittle kiss for my dolly,
  And one 'ittle uzzer for me!'"

God pity the heart that repelled her,
  And the cold hand that turned her away!
And take, from the lips that denied her,
  This answerless prayer of to-day!
Take, Lord, from my mem'ry forever
  That pitiful sob of despair,
And the patter and trip of the little bare feet,
  And the one piercing cry on the stair!

I put by the half-written poem,
  While the pen, idly trailed in my hand,
Writes on, "Had I words to complete it,
  Who'd read it, or who'd understand?"

But the little bare feet on the stairway,
    And the faint, smothered laugh in the hall,
And the eerie-low lisp on the silence,
    Cry up to me over it all.

THE SPHINX.

I KNOW all about the Sphinx —
  I know even what she thinks,
Staring with her stony eyes
Up forever at the skies.

For last night I dreamed that she
Told me all the mystery —
Why for æons mute she sat: —
She was just cut out for that!

IF I KNEW WHAT POETS KNOW.

IF I knew what poets know,
    Would I write a rhyme
Of the buds that never blow
    In the summer time?
Would I sing of golden seeds
Springing up in ironweeds?
And of raindrops turned to snow,
If I knew what poets know?

Did I know what poets do,
    Would I sing a song
Sadder than the pigeon's coo
    When the days are long?
Where I found a heart in pain,
I would make it glad again;
And the false should be the true,
Did I know what poets do.

If I knew what poets know,
　I would find a theme
Sweeter than the placid flow
　Of the fairest dream;
I would sing of love that lives
On the errors it forgives,
And the world would better grow
If I knew what poets know.

IKE WALTON'S PRAYER.

I CRAVE, dear Lord,
   No boundless hoard
  Of gold and gear,
    Nor jewels fine,
    Nor lands, nor kine,
Nor treasure-heaps of anything.—
    Let but a little hut be mine
    Where at the hearthstone I may hear
      The cricket sing,
      And have the shine
  Of one glad woman's eyes to make,
  For my poor sake,
    Our simple home a place divine;—
Just the wee cot—the cricket's chirr—
Love, and the smiling face of her.

I pray not for
Great riches, nor
   For vast estates, and castle-halls,—
   Give me to hear the bare footfalls
      Of children o'er
      An oaken floor,
   New-rinsed with sunshine, or bespread
   With but the tiny coverlet
   And pillow for the baby's head;
And, pray Thou, may
The door stand open and the day
   Send ever in a gentle breeze,
   With fragrance from the locust-trees,
      And drowsy moan of doves, and blur
   Of robin-chirps, and drone of bees,
      With afterhushes of the stir
   Of intermingling sounds, and then
      The good-wife and the smile of her
   Filling the silences again—
         The cricket's call,
            And the wee cot,
         Dear Lord of all,
            Deny me not!

I pray not that
Men tremble at
   My power of place
    And lordly sway,—
I only pray for simple grace
To look my neighbor in the face
   Full honestly from day to day—
Yield me his horny palm to hold,
   And I'll not pray
    For gold;—
The tanned face, garlanded with mirth,
It hath the kingliest smile on earth—
The swart brow, diamonded with sweat,
Hath never need of coronet.
   And so I reach,
    Dear Lord, to Thee,
   And do beseech
    Thou givest me
The wee cot, and the cricket's chirr,
Love, and the glad sweet face of her!

A ROUGH SKETCH.

I CAUGHT, for a second, across the crowd —
Just for a second, and barely that —
A face, pox-pitted and evil-browed,
  Hid in the shade of a slouch-rim'd hat —
    With small, gray eyes, of a look as keen
    As the long, sharp nose that grew between.

And I said: 'Tis a sketch of Nature's own,
  Drawn i' the dark o' the moon, I swear,
On a tatter of Fate that the winds have blown
  Hither and thither and everywhere —
    With its keen little sinister eyes of gray,
    And nose like the beak of a bird of prey!

OUR KIND OF A MAN.

I.

THE kind of a man for you and me!
  He faces the world unflinchingly,
And smites, as long as the wrong resists,
With a knuckled faith and force like fists:
He lives the life he is preaching of,
And loves where most is the need of love;
His voice is clear to the deaf man's ears,
And his face sublime through the blind man's
      tears;
The light shines out where the clouds were dim,
And the widow's prayer goes up for him;
The latch is clicked at the hovel door,
And the sick man sees the sun once more,
And out o'er the barren fields he sees
Springing blossoms and waving trees,
Feeling as only the dying may,
That God's own servant has come that way,

Smoothing the path as it still winds on
Through the golden gate where his loved have
  gone.

II.

The kind of a man for me and you!
However little of worth we do
He credits full, and abides in trust
That time will teach us how more is just.
He walks abroad, and he meets all kinds
Of querulous and uneasy minds,
And, sympathizing, he shares the pain
Of the doubts that rack us, heart and brain;
And, knowing this, as we grasp his hand,
We are surely coming to understand!
He looks on sin with pitying eyes—
E'en as the Lord, since Paradise,—
Else, should we read, though our sins should glow
As scarlet, they shall be white as snow?—
And feeling still, with a grief half glad,
That the bad are as good as the good are bad,
He strikes straight out for the Right—and he
Is the kind of a man for you and me!

THE HARPER.

LIKE a drift of faded blossoms
  Caught in a slanting rain,
His fingers glimpsed down the strings of his harp
  In a tremulous refrain.

Patter, and tinkle, and drip, and drip!
  Ah! but the chords were rainy sweet!
And I closed my eyes and I bit my lip,
  As he played there in the street.

Patter, and drip, and tinkle!
  And there was the little bed
In the corner of the garret,
  And the rafters overhead!

And there was the little window—
  Tinkle, and drip, and drip!—
The rain above, and a mother's love,
  And God's companionship!

OLD AUNT MARY'S.

WASN'T it pleasant, O brother mine,
  In those old days of the lost sunshine
Of youth — when the Saturday's chores were
        through,
And the "Sunday's wood" in the kitchen, too,
And we went visiting, "me and you,"
        Out to Old Aunt Mary's?

It all comes back so clear to-day!
Though I am as bald as you are gray —
Out by the barn-lot, and down the lane,
We patter along in the dust again,
As light as the tips of the drops of the rain,
        Out to Old Aunt Mary's!

We cross the pasture, and through the wood
Where the old gray snag of the poplar stood,
Where the hammering "red-heads" hopped awry,
And the buzzard "raised" in the "clearing"- sky,
And lolled and circled, as we went by
      Out to Old Aunt Mary's.

And then in the dust of the road again;
And the teams we met, and the countrymen;
And the long highway, with sunshine spread
As thick as butter on country bread,
Our cares behind, and our hearts ahead
      Out to Old Aunt Mary's.

Why, I see her now in the open door,
Where the little gourds grew up the sides, and o'er
The clapboard roof!—And her face—ah, me!
Wasn't it good for a boy to see—
And wasn't it good for a boy to be
      Out to Old Aunt Mary's?

And O my brother, so far away,
This is to tell you she waits to-day
To welcome us:—Aunt Mary fell
Asleep this morning, whispering, "Tell
The boys to come!" And all is well
         Out to Old Aunt Mary's.

ILLILEO, the moonlight seemed lost across the
    vales —
The stars but strewed the azure as an armor's
    scattered scales;
The airs of night were quiet as the breath of
    silken sails,
And all your words were sweeter than the notes
    of nightingales.

Illileo Legardi, in the garden there alone,
With your figure carved of fervor, as the Psyche
    carved of stone,
There came to me no murmur of the fountain's
    undertone
So mystically, musically mellow as your own.

You whispered low, Illileo — so low the leaves
    were mute,
And the echoes faltered breathless in your voice's
    vain pursuit;
And there died the distant dalliance of the
    serenader's lute:
And I held you in my bosom as the husk may
    hold the fruit.

Illileo, I listened. I believed you. In my bliss,
What were all the worlds above me since I found
    you thus in this? —
Let them reeling reach to win me — even Heaven
    I would miss,
Grasping earthward! — I would cling here, though
    I clung by just a kiss.

And blossoms should grow odorless — and lilies all
    aghast —
And I said the stars should slacken in their paces
    through the vast,

Ere yet my loyalty should fail enduring to the
    last. —
So vowed I. It is written. It is changeless as
    the past.

Illileo Legardi, in the shade your palace throws
Like a cowl about the singer at your gilded
    porticos,
A moan goes with the music that may vex the
    high repose
Of a heart that fades and crumbles as the crimson
    of a rose,

THE KING.

THEY rode right out of the morning sun —
    A glimmering, glittering cavalcade
Of knights and ladies, and every one
        In princely sheen arrayed;
And the king of them all, O he rode ahead,
With a helmet of gold, and a plume of red
That spurted about in the breeze and bled
        In the bloom of the everglade.

And they rode high over the dewy lawn,
    With brave, glad banners of every hue,
That rolled in ripples, as they rode on
        In splendor, two and two;
And the tinkling links of the golden reins
Of the steeds they rode rang such refrains
As the castanets in a dream of Spain's
        Intensest gold and blue.

And they rode and rode; and the steeds they
      neighed
  And pranced, and the sun on their glossy hides
Flickered and lightened and glanced and played
      Like the moon on rippling tides;
And their manes were silken, and thick and strong,
And their tails were flossy, and fetlock-long,
And jostled in time to the teeming throng,
      And their knightly song besides.

Clank of scabbard and jingle of spur,
  And the fluttering sash of the queen went wild
In the wind, and the proud king glanced at her
      As one at a wilful child,—
And as knight and lady away they flew,
And the banners flapped, and the falcon, too,
And the lances flashed and the bugle blew,
      He kissed his hand and smiled.—

And then, like a slanting sunlit shower,
  The pageant glittered across the plain,
And the turf spun back, and the wildweed flower
      Was only a crimson stain.

And a dreamer's eyes they are downward cast,
As he blends these words with the wailing blast:
"It is the King of the Year rides past!"
And Autumn is here again.

A BRIDE.

"O I AM weary!" she sighed, as her billowy
  Hair she unloosed in a torrent of gold
That rippled and fell o'er a figure as willowy,
  Graceful and fair as a goddess of old:
Over her jewels she flung herself drearily,
  Crumpled the laces that snowed on her breast,
Crushed with her fingers the lily that wearily
  Clung in her hair like a dove in its nest.
      —And naught but her shadowy form in the
          mirror
        To kneel in dumb agony down and weep
          near her!

"Weary?"—of what? Could we fathom the mys-
          tery?—
  Lift up the lashes weighed down by her tears,
And wash with their dews one white face from her
          history,

Set like a gem in the red rust of years?
Nothing will rest her—unless he who died of her
. Strayed from his grave, and, in place of the groom,
Tipping her face, kneeling there by the side of her,
Drained the old kiss to the dregs of his doom.
—And naught but that shadowy form in the
mirror
To kneel in dumb agony down and weep
near her!

THE DEAD LOVER.

TIME is so long when a man is dead!
      Some one sews; and the room is made
Very clean; and the light is shed
      Soft through the window-shade.

Yesterday I thought: "I know
      Just how the bells will sound, and how
The friends will talk, and the sermon go,
      And the hearse-horse bow and bow!"

This is to-day; and I have no thing
      To think of — nothing whatever to do
But to hear the throb of the pulse of a wing
      That wants to fly back to you.

A SONG.

THERE is ever a song somewhere, my dear;
   There is ever a something sings alway:
There's the song of the lark when the skies are clear,
   And the song of the thrush when the skies are gray.
The sunshine showers across the grain,
   And the bluebird trills in the orchard tree;
And in and out, when the eaves drip rain,
   The swallows are twittering ceaselessly.

There is ever a song somewhere, my dear,
   Be the skies above or dark or fair,
There is ever a song that our hearts may hear —
There is ever a song somewhere, my dear —
   There is ever a song somewhere!

There is ever a song somewhere, my dear,
  In the midnight black, or the mid-day blue;
The robin pipes when the sun is here,
  And the cricket chirrups the whole night through.
The buds may blow and the fruit may grow,
  And the autumn leaves drop crisp and sere;
But whether the sun, or the rain, or the snow,
  There is ever a song somewhere, my dear.

WHEN BESSIE DIED.

If from your own the dimpled hands had slipped,
 And ne'er would nestle in your palm again;
If the white feet into the grave had tripped—

WHEN Bessie died—
 We braided the brown hair, and tied
It just as her own little hands
Had fastened back the silken strands
A thousand times — the crimson bit
Of ribbon woven into it
That she had worn with childish pride —
Smoothed down the dainty bow — and cried —
 When Bessie died.

When Bessie died —
We drew the nursery blinds aside,
And, as the morning in the room
Burst like a primrose into bloom,

Her pet canary's cage we hung
Where she might hear him when he sung —
And yet not any note he tried,
Though she lay listening folded-eyed.

When Bessie died —
We writhed in prayer unsatisfied;
We begged of God, and He did smile
In silence on us all the while;
And we did see Him, through our tears,
Enfolding that fair form of hers,
She laughing back against His love
The kisses we had nothing of—
And death to us he still denied,
When Bessie died—
                    When Bessie died.

THE SHOWER.

THE landscape, like the awed face of a child,
   Grew curiously blurred; a hush of death
Fell on the fields, and in the darkened wild
   The zephyr held its breath.

No wavering glamour-work of light and shade
   Dappled the shivering surface of the brook;
The frightened ripples in their ambuscade
   Of willows thrilled and shook.

The sullen day grew darker, and anon
   Dim flashes of pent anger lit the sky;
With rumbling wheels of wrath came rolling on
   The storm's artillery.

The cloud above put on its blackest frown,
    And then, as with a vengeful cry of pain,
The lightning snatched it, ripped and flung it down
    In raveled shreds of rain:

While I, transfigured by some wondrous art,
    Bowed with the thirsty lilies to the sod,
My empty soul brimmed over, and my heart
    Drenched with the love of God.

A LIFE-LESSON.

THERE! little girl; don't cry!
  They have broken your doll, I know;
    And your tea-set blue,
    And your play-house, too,
  Are things of the long ago;
    But childish troubles will soon pass by.—
    There! little girl; don't cry!

There! little girl; don't cry!
  They have broken your slate, I know;
    And the glad, wild ways
    Of your school-girl days
  Are things of the long ago;
    But life and love will soon come by.—
    There! little girl; don't cry!

There! little girl; don't cry!
    They have broken your heart, I know;
    And the rainbow gleams
    Of your youthful dreams
Are things of the long ago;
    But heaven holds all for which you
        sigh.—
    There! little girl; don't cry!

A SCRAWL.

I WANT to sing something—but this is all—
   I try and I try, but the rhymes are dull,
As though they were damp, and the echoes fall
    Limp and unlovable.

Words will not say what I yearn to say—
   They will not walk as I want them to;
But they stumble and fall in the path of the way
    Of my telling my love for you.

Simply take what the scrawl is worth—
   Knowing I love you as sun the sod
On the ripening side of the great round earth
    That swings in the smile of God.

AWAY.

I CAN NOT say, and I will not say
That he is dead.— He is just away!

With a cheery smile, and a wave of the hand,
He has wandered into an unknown land,

And left us dreaming how very fair
It needs must be, since he lingers there.

And you— O you, who the wildest yearn
For the old-time step and the glad return,—

Think of him faring on, as dear
In the love of There as the love of Here;

And loyal still, as he gave the blows
Of his warrior-strength to his country's foes.—

64

Mild and gentle, as he was brave,—
When the sweetest love of his life he gave

To simple things:—Where the violets grew
Pure as the eyes they were likened to,

The touches of his hands have strayed
As reverently as his lips have prayed:

When the little brown thrush that harshly chirred
Was dear to him as the mocking-bird;

And he pitied as much as a man in pain
A writhing honey-bee wet with rain.—

Think of him still as the same, I say:
He is not dead—he is just away!

WHO BIDES HIS TIME.

WHO bides his time, and day by day
   Faces defeat full patiently,
And lifts a mirthful roundelay,
   However poor his fortunes be,—
He will not fail in any qualm
   Of poverty — the paltry dime
It will grow golden in his palm,
   Who bides his time.

Who bides his time — he tastes the sweet
   Of honey in the saltest tear;
And though he fares with slowest feet,
   Joy runs to meet him, drawing near;
The birds are heralds of his cause,
   And like a never-ending rhyme,
The roadsides bloom in his applause,
   Who bides his time.

66

Who bides his time, and fevers not
  In the hot race that none achieves,
Shall wear cool-wreathen laurel, wrought
  With crimson berries in the leaves;
And he shall reign a goodly king,
  And sway his hand o'er every clime,
With peace writ on his signet ring,
  Who bides his time.

FROM THE HEADBOARD OF A GRAVE IN PARAGUAY.

A TROTH, and a grief, and a blessing,
  Disguised them and came this way,—
And one was a promise, and one was a doubt,
  And one was a rainy day.

And they met betimes with this maiden,—
  And the promise it spake and lied,
And the doubt it gibbered and hugged itself,
  And the rainy day—she died.

LAUGHTER HOLDING BOTH HIS SIDES.

AYE, thou varlet! Laugh away!
  All the world's a holiday!
Laugh away, and roar and shout
Till thy hoarse tongue lolleth out!
Bloat thy cheeks, and bulge thine eyes
Unto bursting, pelt thy thighs
With thy swollen palms, and roar
As thou never hast before!
Lustier! wilt thou! peal on peal!
Stiflest? Squat and grind thy heel —
Wrestle with thy loins, and then
Wheeze thee whiles, and whoop again!

SONNETS

PAN.

THIS PAN is but an idle god, I guess,
 Since all the fair midsummer of my dreams
 He loiters listlessly by woody streams,
Soaking the lush glooms up with laziness;
Or drowsing while the maiden-winds caress
 Him prankishly, and powder him with
  gleams
 Of sifted sunshine. And he ever seems
Drugged with a joy unutterable — unless
 His low pipes whistle hints of it far out
Across the ripples to the dragonfly
 That, like a wind-born blossom blown about,
Drops quiveringly down, as though to die —
 Then lifts and wavers on, as if in doubt
 Whether to fan his wings or fly without.

DUSK.

THE frightened herds of clouds across the sky
    Trample the sunshine down, and chase the day
    Into the dusky forest-lands of gray
And sombre twilight. Far, and faint, and high,
The wild goose trails his harrow, with a cry
    Sad as the wail of some poor castaway
    Who sees a vessel drifting far astray
Of his last hope, and lays him down to die.
The children, riotous from school, grow bold,
    And quarrel with the wind whose angry gust
Plucks off the summer-hat, and flaps the fold
    Of many a crimson cloak, and twirls the dust
In spiral shapes grotesque, and dims the gold
    Of gleaming tresses with the blur of rust.

JUNE.

O QUEENLY month of indolent repose!
　　I drink thy breath in sips of rare perfume,
　As in thy downy lap of clover-bloom
I nestle like a drowsy child, and doze
The lazy hours away.　The zephyr throws
　　The shifting shuttle of the summer's loom,
　And weaves a damask-work of gleam and
　　　　gloom
Before thy listless feet:　The lily blows
　A bugle-call of fragrance o'er the glade;
　　And, wheeling into ranks, with plume and
　　　　spear,
　Thy harvest-armies gather on parade;
　　While, faint and far away, yet pure and
　　　　clear,
　A voice calls out of alien lands of shade,—
　　"All hail the Peerless Goddess of the Year!"

SILENCE.

THOUSANDS and thousands of hushed years
    ago,
  Out on the edge of Chaos, all alone
  I stood on peaks of vapor, high upthrown
Above a sea that knew nor ebb nor flow,
Nor any motion won of winds that blow,
  Nor any sound of watery wail or moan,
  Nor lisp of wave, nor wandering undertone
Of any tide lost in the night below.
So still it was, I mind me, as I laid
  My thirsty ear against mine own faint sigh
To drink of that, I sipped it, half afraid
  'Twas but the ghost of a dead voice spilled by
The one starved star that tottered through the
    shade,
  And came tiptoeing toward me down the sky.

TIME.

I.

THE TICKING — ticking — ticking of the clock!
  That vexed me so last night! — "For though
      Time keeps
  Such drowsy watch," I moaned, "he never
      sleeps,
But only nods above the world to mock
Its restless occupant, then rudely rock
  It as the cradle of a babe that weeps!"
  I seemed to see the seconds piled in heaps
Like sand about me; and at every shock
Of the harsh bell, tolling a new hour's birth,
  The sandy pyramids were swirled away
As by a desert-storm that swept the earth
  Stark as a granary floor, whereon the gray
And mist-bedrizzled moon amidst the dearth
  Came crawling, like a sickly child, to lay
  Its pale face next mine own and weep for day.

TIME.

Wait for the morning! Ah! we wait indeed
  For daylight, we who toss about through stress
  Of vacant-armed desires and emptiness
Of all the warm, warm touches that we need,
And the warm kisses upon which we feed
  Our famished lips in fancy! May God bless
  The starved lips of us with but one caress
Warm as the yearning blood our poor hearts
      bleed!
. . . . A wild prayer!—bite thy pillow, praying
      so —
  Toss this side, and whirl that, and moan for
      dawn;
Let the clock's seconds dribble out their woe,
And Time be drained of sorrow! Long ago
  We heard the crowing cock, with answer
      drawn,
  As hoarsely sad at throat as sobs. . . . . Pray
      on!

SLEEP.

THOU drowsy god, whose blurred eyes, half
    awink,
  Muse on me,— drifting out upon thy dreams,
  I lave my soul as in enchanted streams,
Where reveling satyrs pipe along the brink,
And, tipsy with the melody they drink,
  Uplift their dangling hooves and down the
    beams
  Of sunshine dance like motes. Thy languor
    seems
An ocean-depth of love wherein I sink
  Like some fond Argonaut, right willingly,—
Because of wooing eyes upturned to mine,
  And siren-arms that coil their sorcery
About my neck, with kisses so divine,
  The heavens reel above me, and the sea
  Swallows and licks its wet lips over me.

HER HAIR.

THE beauty of her hair bewilders me —
   Pouring adown the brow, its cloven tide
   Swirling about the ears on either side,
And storming round the neck tumultuously:
Or like the lights of old antiquity
     Through mullioned windows, in cathedrals
       wide,
     Spilled moltenly o'er figures deified
In chastest marble, nude of drapery.
And so I love it.— Either unconfined;
     Or plaited in close braidings manifold;
Or smoothly drawn; or indolently twined
     In careless knots whose coilings come
       unrolled
At any lightest kiss; or by the wind
   Whipped out in flossy ravelings of gold.

DEARTH.

I HOLD your trembling hand to-night—and yet
  I may not know what wealth of bliss is mine,
   My heart is such a curious design
Of trust and jealousy! Your eyes are wet—
So must I think they jewel some regret,—
   And lo, the loving arms that round me twine
   Cling only as the tendrils of a vine
Whose fruit has long been gathered: I forget,
  While crimson clusters of your kisses press
    Their wine out on my lips, my royal fare
Of rapture, since blind fancy needs must guess
    They once poured out their sweetness
        otherwhere,
  With fuller flavoring of happiness
    Then e'en your broken sobs may now declare.

A VOICE FROM THE FARM.

IT is my dream to have you here with me,
　Out of the heated city's dust and din —
　　Here where the colts have room to gambol in,
And kine to graze, in clover to the knee.
I want to see your wan face happily
　Lit with the wholesome smiles that have not
　　　been
　In use since the old games you used to win
When we pitched horseshoes: And I want to be
　At utter loaf with you in this dim land
　　Of grove and meadow, while the crickets
　　　make
　　Our own talk tedious, and the bat wields
His bulky flight, as we cease converse, and
　In a dusk like velvet smoothly take
　　Our way toward home across the dewy
　　　fields.

WHEN SHE COMES HOME.

WHEN she comes home again! A thousand
       ways
   I fashion, to myself, the tenderness
   Of my glad welcome: I shall tremble—yes;
And touch her, as when first in the old days
I touched her girlish hand, nor dared upraise
   Mine eyes, such was my faint heart's sweet
       distress.
   Then silence: And the perfume of her dress:
The room will sway a little, and a haze
   Cloy eyesight—soulsight, even—for a space:
And tears—yes; and the ache here in the throat,
   To know that I so ill deserve the place
Her arms make for me; and the sobbing note
   I stay with kisses, ere the tearful face
   Again is hidden in the old embrace.

ART AND LOVE.

HE faced his canvas (as a seer whose ken
  Pierces the crust of this existence through)
  And smiled beyond on that his genius knew
Ere mated with his being. Conscious then
Of his high theme alone, he smiled again
  Straight back upon himself in many a hue,
    And tint, and light, and shade, which slowly
      grew
Enfeatured of a fair girl's face, as when
  First time she smiles for love sake with no
    fear.
So wrought he, witless that behind him leant
  A woman, with old features, dim and sere,
  And glamoured eyes that felt the brimming
    tear,
And with a voice, like some sad instrument,
  That sighing said, "I'm dead there; love me
    here!"

IN DIALECT

PAP'S got his patent-right, and rich as all
          creation;
  But where's the peace and comfort that we all
          had before?
Le's go a-visitin' back to Griggsby's Station—
  Back where we ust to be so happy and so pore!

The likes of us a-livin' here! It's jest a mortal
          pity
  To see us in this great big house, with cyarpets
          on the stairs,
And the pump right in the kitchen! And the
          city! city! city!—
  And nothin' but the city all around us
          ever'wheres!

Climb clean above the roof and look from the
    steeple,
  And never see a robin, nor a beech or ellum
    tree !
And right here in ear-shot of at least a thousan'
    people,
  And none that neighbors with us, or we want
    to go and see !

Le's go a-visitin' back to Griggsby's Station —
  Back where the latch-string's a-hangin' from the
    door,
And ever' neighbor 'round the place is dear as a
    relation —
  Back where we ust to be so happy and so
    pore !

I want to see the Wiggenses, the whole kit and
    bilin',
  A drivin' up from Shallor Ford to stay the
    Sunday through ;
And I want to see 'em hitchin' at their
    son-in-law's and pilin'
  Out there at 'Lizy Ellen's like they ust to do !

I want to see the piece-quilts the Jones girls is
            makin' ;
    And I want to pester Laury 'bout their
            freckled hired hand,
And joke her 'bout the widower she come purt'
            nigh a-takin',
    Till her pap got his pension 'lowed in time to
            save his land.

Le's go a-visitin' back to Griggsby's Station —
    Back where they's nothin' aggervatin' anymore,
Shet away safe in the woods around the old
            location —
    Back where we ust to be so happy and so
            pore !

I want to see Marindy and he'p her with her
            sewin',
    And hear her talk so lovin' of her man that's
            dead and gone,
And stand up with Emanuel to show me how
            he's growin',
    And smile as I have saw her 'fore she put her
            mournin' on.

And I want to see the Samples, on the old lower
    eighty —
  Where John our oldest boy, he was tuk and
    burried — for
His own sake and Katy's, — and I want to cry
    with Katy
  As she reads all his letters over, writ from The
    War.

What's in all this grand life and high situation,
  And nary a pink nor hollyhawk bloomin' at
    the door?—
Le's go a-visitin' back to Griggsby's Station —
  Back where we ust to be so happy and so
    pore!

KNEE-DEEP IN JUNE.

I.

TELL you what I like the best —
    'Long about knee-deep in June,
    'Bout the time strawberries melts
    On the vine, — some afternoon
Like to jes' git out and rest,
    And not work at nothin' else!

II.

Orchard's where I'd ruther be —
Need n't fence it in fer me! —
    Jes' the whole sky overhead,
    And the whole airth underneath —
    Sorto' so's a man kin breathe
Like he ort, and kindo' has
Elbow-room to keerlessly
    Sprawl out len'thways on the grass

Where the shadders thick and soft
As the kivvers on the bed
    Mother fixes in the loft
Allus, when they's company!

III.

Jes' a sorto' lazein' there —
    S'lazy, 'at you peek and peer
        Through the wavin' leaves above,
        Like a feller 'ats in love
    And don't know it, ner don't keer!
    Ever'thing you hear and see
        Got some sort o' interest —
        Maybe find a bluebird's nest
    Tucked up there conveenently
    Fer the boys 'ats apt to be
    Up some other apple-tree!
Watch the swallers skootin' past
'Bout as peert as you could ast;
    Er the Bobwhite raise and whiz
    Where some other's whistle is.

IV.

Ketch a shadder down below,
And look up to find the crow;
Er a hawk away up there,
'Pearantly froze in the air! —
  Hear the old hen squawk, and squat
  Over every chick she's got,
Suddent-like! — And she knows where
  That-air hawk is, well as you! —
  You jes' bet yer life she do! —
    Eyes a-glitterin' like glass,
    Waitin' till he makes a pass!

v.

Pee-wees' singin', to express
  My opinion's second class,
Yit you'll hear 'em more er less;
  Sapsucks gittin' down to biz,
Weedin' out the lonesomeness;
  Mr. Bluejay, full o' sass,
    In them base-ball clothes o' his,
Sportin' 'round the orchard jes'

Like he owned the premises!
  Sun out in the fields kin sizz,
But flat on yer back, I guess,
  In the shade's where glory is!
    That's jes' what I'd like to do
    Stiddy fer a year er two!

VI.

Plague! ef they aint sompin' in
Work 'at kindo' goes ag'in
  My convictions! —'long about
  Here in June especially! —
  Under some old apple tree,
    Jes' a-restin' through and through,
I could git along without
  Nothin' else at all to do
  Only jes' a-wishin' you
Was a-gittin' there like me,
And June was eternity!

VII.

Lay out there and try to see
Jes' how lazy you kin be! —

Tumble round and souse yer head
In the clover-bloom, er pull
 Yer straw hat acrost yer eyes,
 And peek through it at the skies,
Thinkin' of old chums 'ats dead,
 Maybe, smilin' back at you
In betwixt the beautiful
  Clouds o' gold and white and
   blue! —
Month a man kin railly love —
June, you know, I'm talkin' of!

VIII.

March aint never nothin' new! —
Aprile's altogether too
 Brash fer me! and May — I jes'
 'Bominate its promises, —
  Little hints o' sunshine and
Green around the timber-land —
A few blossoms, and a few
Chip-birds, and a sprout er two —
Drap asleep, and it turns in
'Fore daylight and snows agin! —

But when June comes — Clear my throat
    With wild honey! Rench my hair
In the dew! and hold my coat!
      Whoop out loud! and throw my hat! —
June wants me, and I'm to spare!
Spread them shadders anywhere,
I'll git down and waller there,
    And obleeged to you at that!

WHEN THE HEARSE COMES BACK.

A THING 'at's 'bout as tryin' as a healthy man
   kin meet
Is some poor feller's funeral a-joggin' 'long the
   street:
The slow hearse and the hosses — slow enough, to
   say the least,
Fer to even tax the patience of the gentleman
   deceased!
The slow scrunch of the gravel — and the slow
   grind of the wheels,—
The slow, slow go of ev'ry woe 'at ev'rybody
   feels!
So I ruther like the contrast when I hear the
   whiplash crack
A quickstep fer the hosses,
     When the
        Hearse
          Comes
            Back!

Meet it goin' to'rds the cemet'ry, you'll want to
      drap yer eyes—
But ef the plumes don't fetch you, it'll ketch you
      otherwise—
You'll haf to see the caskit, though you'd ort to
      look away,
And 'conomize and save yer sighs for any other
      day!
Yer sympathizin' won't wake up the sleeper from
      his rest—
Yer tears won't thaw them hands o' his 'at's froze
      acrost his breast!
And this is why—when airth and sky's a-gittin'
      blurred and black—
I like the flash and hurry
      When the
            Hearse
                  Comes
                        Back!

It's not 'cause I don't 'preciate it aint no time
      fer jokes,
Ner 'cause I' got no common human feelin's fer
      the folks;—

I've went to funerals myse'f, and took on some,
      perhaps,
Fer my heart's 'bout as mall'able as any other
      chap's,—
I've buried father, mother — but I'll haf to jes'
      git you
To "excuse *me*," as the feller says.— The p'int
      I'm drivin' to
Is, simply, when we're plum' broke down and all
      knocked out a'whack,
It he'ps to shape us up, like,
      When the
             Hearse
               Comes
                  Back!

The idy! wadin' round here over shoe-mouth deep
      in woe,
When they's a graded 'pike o' joy and sunshine,
      don't you know!
When evenin' strikes the pastur', cows'll pull out
      fer the bars,
And skittish-like from out the night'll prance the
      happy stars.

And so when my time comes to die, and I've got
    ary friend
'At wants expressed my last request — I'll, mebby,
    rickommend
To drive slow, ef they haf to, goin' 'long the
    out'ard track,
But I'll smile and say, " You speed 'em
    When the
           Hearse
              Comes
                Back ! "

A CANARY AT THE FARM.

FOLKS has ben to town and Sahry
 Fetched 'er home a pet canary,—
And of all the blame', contrary,
    Aggervatin' things alive!
I love music — that's I love it
When its *free* — and plenty of it; —
But I kindo' git above it,
    At a dollar-eighty-five!

Reason's plain as I'm a-sayin',—
Jes' the idy, now, o' layin'
Out yer money, and a-payin'
    Fer a willer-cage and bird,
When the medder-larks is wingin'
Round you, and the woods is ringin'
With the beautifullest singin'
    That a mortal ever heard!

Sahry's sot, tho',—so I tell her
He's a purty little feller,
With his wings o' creamy-yeller,
    And his eyes keen as a cat;
And the twitter o' the critter
'Pears to absolutely glitter!
Guess I'll haf to go and git her
    A high-priceter cage 'n that!

A LIZ-TOWN HUMORIST.

SETTIN' round the stove, last night,
 Down at Wess's store, was me
And Mart Strimples, Tunk, and White,
 And Doc Bills, and two er three
Fellers of the Mudsock tribe
No use tryin' to describe!
And says Doc, he says, says he,—
"Talkin' 'bout good things to eat,
 Ripe mushmillon's hard to beat!"

I chawed on. And Mart he 'lowed
 Wortermillon beat the mush.—
"Red," he says, "and juicy — Hush! —
 I'll jes' leave it to the crowd!"
Then a Mudsock chap, says he,—
"Punkin's good enough fer me —
 Punkin pies, I mean," he says,—
"Them beats millons! What say, Wess?"

I chawed on. And Wess says,—" Well,
You jes' fetch that wife of mine
All yer wortermillon-*rine*,
And she'll bile it down a spell—
In with sorgum, I suppose,
And what else, Lord only knows!—
But I'm here to tell all hands,
Them p'serves meets my demands!"

I chawed on. And White he says,—
" Well, I'll jes' stand in with Wess—
I'm no hog!" And Tunk says,—"I
Guess I'll pastur' out on pie
With the Mudsock boys!" says he;
"Now what's yourn?" he says to me:
I chawed on—fer -quite a spell—
Then I speaks up, slow and dry,—
" Jes' tobacker!" I-says-I.—
And you'd orto' heerd 'em yell!

KINGRY'S MILL.

ON old Brandywine — about
    Where White's Lots is now laid out,
And the old crick narries down
To the ditch that splits the town, —
Kingry's Mill stood: Hardly see
Where the old dam ust to be;
Shallor, long, dry trought o' grass
Where the old race ust to pass!

That's ben forty years ago —
Forty years of frost and snow —
Forty years of shade and shine
Sence them boyhood days o' mine! —
All the old landmarks o' town,
Changed about, er rotted down!
Where's the tanyard? Where's the'still?
Tell me where's old Kingry's Mill?

Don't seem furder back, to me,
I'll be dogg'd! than yisterdy,
Sence us fellers, in bare feet
And straw hats, went through the wheat,
Cuttin' crost the shortest shoot
Fer that-air old ellum-root
Jest above the mill-dam, where
The blame' cars now crosses there!

Through the willers down the crick
We could see the old mill stick
Its red gable up, as if
It jest knowed we'd stol'd the skiff!
See the winders in the sun
Blink like they was wonderun'
What the miller ort to do
With sich boys as me and you!

But old Kingry! — who could fear
That old chap, with all his cheer? —
Leanin' at the winder-sill,
Er the half-door of the mill,

Swoppin' lies, and pokin' fun
'N jigglin' like his hoppers done,
Laughin' grists o' gold and red
Right out o' the wagon-bed!

What did HE keer where we went? —
"Jest keep out o' devilment,
 And don't fool around the belts,
 Bolts, ner burrs, ner nothin' else
'Bout the blame *machinery*,
 And that's all I ast!" says-ee.
Then we'd climb the stairs, and play
In the bran-bins half the day!

Rickollect the dusty wall,
And the spider-webs, and all!
Rickollect the trimblin' spout
Where the meal come josslin' out —
Stand and comb yer fingers through
The fool-truck an hour er two —
Felt so sort o' warm-like and
Soothin' to a feller's hand!

107

Climb, high up above the stream,
And "coon" out the wobbly beam
And peek down from out the lof'
Where the weatherboards was off—
Gee-mun-*nee*! w'y, it takes grit
Even jest to think of it!—
Lookin' 'way down there below
On the worter roarin' so!

Rickollect the flume, and wheel,
And the worter, slosh and reel,
And jest ravel out in froth
Flossier'n satin cloth!
Rickollect them paddles jest
Knock the bubbles galley-west,
And plunge under, and come up,
Drippin' like a worter-pup!

And, to see them old things gone
That I onc't was bettin' on,
In rale pint o' fact, I feel
Kindo' like that worter-wheel,—

Sorto' drippy-like and wet
Round the eyes — but paddlin' yet,
And, in mem'ry, loafin' still
Down around old Kingry's Mill!

JONEY.

HAD a hare-lip — Joney had :
  Spiled his looks, and Joney knowed it;
Fellers tried to bore him, bad —
But, ef ever he got mad,
  He kep' still and never showed it.
'Druther have his mouth, all pouted
  And split up, and like it wuz,
Than the ones 'at laughed about it. —
  Purty is as purty does!

Had to listen ruther clos't
  'Fore you knowed what he wuz givin'
You; and yet, without no boast
Joney he wuz jes' the most
  Entertainin' talker livin'!
Take the Scriptures and run through 'em,
  Might say, like a' auctionier,
And 'ud argy and review 'em
  'At wuz beautiful to hear!

Hare-lip and inpediment,
  Both wuz bad, and both agin him—
But the old folks where he went,
'Peared like, knowin' his intent,
  'Scused his mouth for what wuz in him.
And *the childern* all loved Joney—
  And he loved 'em back, you bet!—
Put their arms around him——on'y
  None had ever kissed him yet!

In young company, someway,
  Boys 'ud grin at one-another
On the sly; and girls 'ud lay
Low, with nothin' much to say,
  Er leave Joney with their mother.
Many and many a time he's fetched 'em
  Candy by the paper-sack,
And turned right around and ketched 'em
  Makin' mouths behind his back!

S'prised, sometimes, the slurs he took.—
  Chap said onc't his mouth looked sorter
Like a fish's mouth 'ud look
When he'd ben jerked off the hook
  And plunked back into the worter.—
Same durn feller—its su'prisin',
  But it's facts—'at stood and cherred
From the bank that big baptizin'
  'Pike-bridge accident occurred!

Cherred fer Joney while he give
  Life to little childern drowndin'!
Which wuz fittenest to live—
Him 'at cherred, er him 'at div'
  And saved thirteen lives? . . . They
        found one
Body, three days later, floated
  Down the by-o, eight mile' south,
All so colored-up and bloated—
  On'y knowed him by his mouth!

Had a hare-lip — Joney had —
    Folks 'at filed apast all knowed it —
Them 'at ust to smile looked sad,
But ef HE thought good er bad,
    He kep' still and never showed it.
'Druther have that mouth, all pouted
    And split up, and like it wuz,
Than the ones 'at laughed about it.
    Purty is as purty does!

NOTHIN' TO SAY.

NOTHIN' to say, my daughter! Nothin' at all
    to say! —
Gyrls that's in love, I've noticed, ginerly has their
    way!
Yer mother did, afore you, when her folks
    objected to me —
Yit here I am, and here you air; and yer
    mother — where is she?

You look lots like yer mother: Purty much
    same in size;
And about the same complected; and favor about
    the eyes:
Like her, too, about her *livin'* here,—because *she*
    couldn't stay:
It'll 'most seem like you was dead — like her! —
    but I hain't got nothin' to say!

She left you her little Bible — writ yer name
  acrost the page —
And left her ear-bobs fer you, ef ever you come
  of age.
I've allus kep' 'em and gyuarded 'em, but ef yer
  goin' away —
Nothin' to say, my daughter! Nothin' at all to say!

You don't rikollect her, I reckon? No; you
  wasn't a year old then!
And now yer — how old air you? W'y, child,
  not "twenty!" When?
And yer nex' birthday's in Aprile? and you want
  to git married that day?
. . . . I wisht yer mother was livin'! — but — I
  hain't got nothin' to say!

Twenty year! and as good a gyrl as parent ever
  found!
There's a straw ketched onto yer dress there — I'll
  bresh it off — turn round.
(Her mother was jes' twenty when us two run
  away!)
Nothin' to say, my daughter! Nothin' at all to say!

LIKE HIS MOTHER USED TO MAKE.

"UNCLE JAKE'S PLACE," ST. JO, MO., 1874.

" I WAS born in Indiany," says a stranger,
    lank and slim,
As us fellers in the restarunt was kindo' guyin'
    him,
And Uncle Jake was slidin' him another
    punkin pie
And a' extry cup o' coffee, with a twinkle in
    his eye,—
" I was born in Indiany — more'n forty year'
    ago —
And I hain't ben back in twenty — and I'm
    workin' back'ards slow;
But I've et in ever' restarunt twixt here and
    Santy Fee,
And I want to state this coffee tastes like gittin'
    home, to me!

"Pour us out another, Daddy," says the feller,
  warmin' up,
  A-speakin' 'crost a saucerful, as Uncle tuck his
    cup,—
"When I seed yer sign out yander," he went on,
  to Uncle Jake,—
" 'Come in and git some coffee like yer mother
    used to make'—
  I thought of *my* old mother, and the Posey
    county farm,
And me a little kid agin, a-hangin' in her arm,
As she set the pot a-bilin', broke the eggs and
    poured 'em in"—
And the feller kindo' halted, with a trimble in
    his chin:

And Uncle Jake he fetched the feller's coffee
    back, and stood
As solemn, fer a minute, as a' undertaker
    would ;
Then he sorto' turned and tiptoed to'rds the
    kitchen door — and next,
Here comes his old wife out with him, a-rubbin'
    of her specs —

117

And she rushes fer the stranger, and she
    hollers out, "It's him!—
Thank God we've met him comin'!—Don't you
    know yer mother, Jim?"
And the feller, as he grabbed her, says,—
    "You bet I hain't forgot—
But," wipin' of his eyes, says he, "yer coffee's
    mighty hot!"

THE TRAIN-MISSER.

'LL WHERE in the world my eyes has bin —
  Ef I haint missed that train agin!
Chuff! and whistle! and toot! and ring!
But blast and blister the dasted train! —
How it does it I can't explain!
Git here thirty-five minutes before
The dern thing's due! — and, drat the thing!
It'll manage to git past — shore!

The more I travel around, the more
I got no sense! — To stand right here
And let it beat me! 'Ll ding my melts!
I got no gumption, ner nothin' else!
Ticket Agent's a dad-burned bore! —
Sell you a ticket's all they keer! —

119

Ticket Agents ort to all be
Prosecuted — and that's jes' what! —
How'd I know which train's fer me?
And how'd I know which train was not?—
Goern and comin' and gone astray,
And backin' and switchin' ever'-which-way!

Ef I could jes' sneak round behind
Myse'f, where I could git full swing,—
I'd lift my coat, and kick, by jing!
Till I jes' got jerked up and fined!—
Fer here I stood, as a dern fool's apt
To, and let that train jes' chuff and choo
Right apast me — and mouth jes' gapped
Like a blamed old sandwitch warped in two!

GRANNY.

GRANNY'S come to our house,
    And ho! my lawzy-daisy!
All the childern round the place
    Is ist a-runin' crazy!
Fetched a cake fer little Jake,
    And fetched a pie fer Nanny,
And fetched a pear fer all the pack
    That runs to kiss ther Granny!

Lucy Ellen's in her lap,
    And Wade, and Silas Walker,
Both's a-ridin' on her foot,
    And 'Pollos on the rocker;
And Marthy's twins, from Aunt Marin's,
    And little orphant Anny,
All's a-eatin' gingerbread
    And giggle-un at Granny!

Tells us all the fairy tales
   Ever thought er wundered —
And 'bundance o' other stories —
   Bet she knows a hunderd! —
Bob's the one fer "Whittington,"
   And "Golden Locks" for Fanny!
Hear 'em laugh and clap ther hands,
   Listenin' at Granny!

"Jack the Giant-Killer"'s good —
   And "Bean-stalk"'s another —
So's the one of Cinderell'
   And her old godmother; —
That un's best of all the rest —
   Bestest one of any, —
Where the mices scampers home
   Like we runs to Granny!

Granny's come to our house,
   Ho! my lawzy-daisy!
All the childern round the place
   Is ist a-runnin' crazy!

Fetched a cake fer little Jake,
  And fetched a pie fer Nanny,
And fetched a pear fer all the pack
  That runs to kiss ther Granny!

OLD OCTOBER.

OLD OCTOBER'S purt' nigh gone,
And the frosts is comin' on
Little heavier every day —
Like our hearts is thataway!
Leaves is changin' overhead
Back from green, to gray and red,
Brown, and yeller, with their stems
Loosenin' on the oaks and e'ms;
And the balance of the trees
Gittin' balder every breeze —
Like the heads we're scratchin' on!
Old October's purt' nigh gone.

I love Old October so,
I can't bear to see her go —
Seems to me like losin' some
Old-home relative, er chum —
'Pears like sorto' settin' by
Some old friend 'at sigh by sigh

Was a-passin' out o' sight
Into everlastin' night!
Hickernuts a feller hears
Rattlin' down is more like tears
Drappin' on the leaves below —
I love Old October so!

Can't tell what it is about
Old October knocks me out! —
I sleep well enough at night —
And the blamedest appetite
Ever mortal man possessed, —
Last thing et, it tastes the best! —
Warnuts, butternuts, pawpaws,
Iles and limbers up my jaws
Fer raal service, sich as new
Pork, spareribs, and sausage, too. —
Yit, fer all, they's somepin' 'bout
Old October knocks me out!

JIM.

HE was jes' a plain, ever'-day, all-round kind of
      a jour.,
    Consumpted-lookin' — but la!
The jokeiest, wittiest, story-tellin', song-singin',
      laughin'est, jolliest
    Feller you ever saw!
Worked at jes' coarse work, but you kin bet he
      was fine enough in his talk,
    And his feelin's too!
Lordy! ef he was on'y back on his bench agin
      to-day, a-carryin' on
    Like he ust to do!

Any shop-mate'll tell you there never was, on top
      o' dirt,
    A better feller'n Jim!
You want a favor, and couldn't git it anywheres
      else —
    You could git it o' him!

Most free-heartedest man thataway in the world, I
        guess!
      Give up ever' nickel he's worth —
And, ef you'd a-wanted it, and named it to him,
        and it was his,
      He'd a-give you the earth!

Allus a-reachin' out, Jim was, and a he'pin' some
        Pore feller onto his feet —
He'd a-never a-keered how hungry he was hisse'f,
      So's *the feller* got somepin' to eat!
Didn't make no difference at all to him how *he*
        was dressed,
      He ust to say to me,—
" You togg out a tramp purty comfortable in
        winter time, a-huntin' a job,
      And he'll git along! " says he.

Jim didn't have, ner never could git ahead so
        overly much
      O' this world's goods at a time.—
'Fore now I've saw him, more'n onc't, lend a
        dollar, and haf' to, more'n likely,
      Turn round and borry a dime!

Mebby laugh and joke about it hisse'f fer a
    while — then jerk his coat,
        And kindo' square his chin,
Tie on his apern, and squat hisse'f on his old
    shoe-bench,
        And go to peggin' agin!

Patientest feller, too, I reckon', at ever jes'
    naturely
        Coughed hisse'f to death!
Long enough after his voice was lost he'd laugh
    in a whisper and say
        He could git ever'thing but his breath —
"You fellers," he'd sorto' twinkle his eyes and say,
    "Is a-pilin onto me
A mighty big debt for that-air little weak-chested
    ghost o'mine to pack
        Through all Eternity!"

Now there was a man 'at jes' 'peared like, to me,
    'At ortn't *a-never* a-died!
"But death hain't a-showin' no favors," the old
    boss said,
        "On'y to Jim!" and cried:

And Wigger, who puts up the best sewed-work
        in the shop,
    Er the whole blame neighborhood,
He says, "When God made Jim, I bet you He
        didn't do anything else that day
    But jes' set around and feel good!"

A TALE OF THE AIRLY DAYS.

OH! TELL ME a tale of the airly days—
　　Of the times as they ust to be;
"Piller Of Fire," and "Shakspeare's Plays,"
　　Is a 'most too deep fer me!
I want plain facts, and I want plain words,
　　Of the good old-fashioned ways,
When speech run free as the songs of birds—
　　'Way back in the airly days.

Tell me a tale of the timber-lands,
　　And the old-time pioneers—
Somepin' a pore man understands
　　With his feelins', well as ears:
Tell of the old log house,—about
　　The loft, and the puncheon floor—
The old fire-place, with the crane swung out,
　　And the latch-string through the door.

Tell of the things jest like they wuz —
  They don't need no excuse!
Don't tetch'em up like the poets does,
  Till they're all too fine fer use!
Say they wuz 'leven in the family —
  Two beds and the chist below,
And the trundle-beds 'at each helt three;
  And the clock and the old bureau.

Then blow the horn at the old back door
  Till the echoes all halloo,
And the childern gethers home onc't more,
  Jest as they ust to do;
Blow fer Pap till he hears and comes,
  With Tomps and Elias, too,
A-marchin' home, with the fife and drums,
  And the old Red White and Blue!

Blow and blow—till the sound draps low
  As the moan of the whipperwill,
And wake up Mother, and Ruth, and Jo,
  All sleepin' at Bethel Hill;

Blow and call till the faces all
　Shine out in the back-log's blaze,
And the shadders dance on the old hewed wall,
　As they did in the airly days.

TO ROBERT BURNS.

SWEET SINGER, that I loe .the maist
   O' ony, sin' wi' eager haste
I smacket bairn-lips ower the taste
      O' hinnied sang,
I hail thee, though a blessed ghaist
      In Heaven lang!

For, weel I ken, nae cantie phrase,
Nor courtly airs, nor lairdly ways,
Could gar me freer blame, or praise,
      Or proffer hand,
Where "Rantin' Robbie" and his lays
      Thegither stand.

And sae these hamely lines I send,
Wi' jinglin' words at ilka end,

In echo of the sangs that wend
   Frae thee to me
Like simmer-brooks, wi' mony a bend
   O' wimplin' glee.

In fancy, as wi' dewy een,
I part the clouds aboon the scene
Where thou wast born, and peer atween,
   I see nae spot
In a' the Hielands half sae green
   And unforgot!

I see nae storied castle-hall,
Wi' banners flauntin' ower the wall,
And serf and page in ready call,
   Sae grand to me
As ane puir cotter's hut, wi' all
   Its poverty.

There where the simple daisy grew
Sae bonnie sweet, and modest, too,

Thy liltin' filled its wee head fu'
     O' sic a grace,
It aye is weepin' tears o' dew
     Wi' droopit face.

Frae where the heather bluebells fling
Their sangs o' fragrance to the Spring,
To where the lavrock soars to sing,
     Still lives thy strain,
For a' the birds are twittering
     Sangs like thine ain.

And aye, by light o' sun or moon,
By banks o' Ayr, or Bonnie Doon,
The waters lilt nae tender tune
     But sweeter seems
Because they poured their limpid rune
     Through a' thy dreams.

Wi' brimmin' lip, and laughin' ee,
Thou shookest even Grief wi' glee,

Yet had nae niggart sympathy
      Where Sorrow bowed,
But gavest a' thy tears as free
      As a' thy gowd.

And sae it is we loe thy name
To see bleeze up wi' sic a flame,
That a' pretentious stars o' fame
      Maun blink asklent,
To see how simple worth may shame
      Their brightest glent.

A NEW YEAR'S TIME AT WILLARDS'S.

I.

THE HIRED MAN TALKS.

THERE'S old man Willards; an' his wife;
  An' Marg'et — S'repty's sister; — an'
    There's me — an' I'm the hired man,
An' Tomps McClure, you bet yer life!

Well, now, old Willards haint so bad,
Considerin' the chance he's had,
Of course, he's rich, an' sleeps an' eats
  Whenever he's a mind to: Takes
An' leans back in the Amen-seats,
  An' thanks the Lord fer all he makes —
That's purty much all folks has got
Ag'inst the old man, like as not!
But there's his woman — jes' the turn
Of them-air two wild girls o' hern —
  Marg'et an' S'repty — allus in
Fer any cuttin'-up concern —
  Church festibals, an' foolishin'

Round Christmas trees, an' New Year's sprees —
    Set up to watch the Old Year go
An' New Year come — sich things as these;
    An' turkey dinners, don't you know!
S'repty 's younger, an' more gay,
    An' purtier, an' finer dressed
Than Marg'et is — but Lawsy-day!
    She haint the independentest! —
"Take care!" old Willards used to say,
"Take care! Let Marg'et have her way,
    An' S'repty, you go off an' play
On your melodeum!"—But best
    Of all comes Tomps! An' I'll be bound,
Ef he haint jes' the beatin'est
    Young chap in all the country round!
        Ef you knowed Tomps you'd like him,
            shore!
    They haint no man on top o' ground
        Walks into my affections more! —
An' all the settlement'll say
That Tomps was liked jes' thataway
    By ever'body, till he tuck
        A shine to S'repty Willards.—Then
    You'd orto' see the old man "buck,"

An' h'ist hisse'f, an' paw the dirt,
    An' hint that common workin'-men
That didn't want their feelin's hurt,
    Had better hunt fer "comp'ny" where
    The folks was pore an' didn't care! —
The pine-blank facts is,—the old man,
  Last Christmas was a year ago,
    Found out some presents Tomps had got
    Fer S'repty, an' hit made him hot —
Set down an' tuck his pen in hand
  An' writ to Tomps an' told him so
    On legal cap, in white an' black,
An' give him jes' to understand
"No Christmas-gifts o' 'lilly-white'
    An' bear's-ile could fix matters right,"
    An' wropped 'em up an' sent 'em back!
Well, S'repty cried and snuffled round
  Consid'able. But Marg'et she
Toed out another sock, an' wound
  Her knittin' up an' drawed the tea,
    An' then set on the supper things,
An' went up in the loft an' dressed —
An' through it all you'd never guessed
    What she was up to! An' she brings

Her best hat with her an' her shawl,
An' gloves, an' redicule, an' all,
An' injirubbers, an' comes down
An' tells 'em she's a-goin' to town
    To he'p the Christmas goin's-on
Her church got up. An' go she does —
The best hosswoman ever was!
    "An' what'll WE do while you're gone?"
The old man says, a-tryin' to be
Agreeable. "Oh! *you?*" says she, —
"*You* kin jaw S'repty, like you did,
    An' slander Tomps!" An' off she rid!

    Now, this is all I'm goin' to tell
        Of this here story — that is, I
            Have done my very level best
    As fer as this, an' here I "dwell,"
        As auctioneers says, winkin' sly:
            Hits old man Willards tells the rest.

THE OLD MAN TALKS.

Adzackly jes' one year ago,
    This New Year's day, Tomps comes to me —

In my own house, an' while the folks
　　Was gittin' dinner,—an' he pokes
His nose right in, an' says, says he:
"I got yer note — an' read it *slow!*
　　You don't like *me*, ner I don't *you*,"
He says,—"we're even there, you know!
　　But you've said, furder, that no gal
　　Of yourn kin marry me, er shall,
An' I'd best shet off comin', too!"
An' then he says,—"Well them's YOUR views,
　　But, havin' talked with S'repty, we
Have both agreed to disagree
　　With your peculiar notions some,
An' that's the reason I refuse
　　To quit a-comin' here, but come —
Not fer to threat, ner raise no skeer,
An' spile yer turkey-dinner here,—
　　But, jes' fer S'repty's sake, to sheer
Yer New Year's.　Shall I take a cheer?"

Well, blame-don! ef I ever see
　　Sich impidence!　I couldn't say
Not nary word!　But mother she
　　Sot out a cheer fer Tomps, an' they

Shuck hands an' turned their back on me.
Then I riz — mad as mad could be —
    But Marg'et says,—"Now, Pap!   you set
    Right where you're settin'!   Don't you fret!
An' Tomps, you warm yer feet!" says she,
    "An' throw yer mitts an' comfort 'on
    The bed there!   Where is S'repty gone? —
    The cabbage is a-scortchin'!   Ma,
    Stop cryin' there an' stir the slaw!"
Well! — what was *Mother cryin'* fer? —
    I half riz up — but Marg'et's chin
    Hit squared — an' I set down agin —
I allus *was* afeared o' her —
I was, by jucks!   So there I set,
Betwixt a sinkin'-chill an' sweat,
An' scuffled with my wrath, an' shet
My teeth to mighty tight, you bet!
    An' yit, fer all that I could do,
I eeched to jes' git up an' whet
    The carvin'-knife a rasp er two
    On Tomps's ribs — an' so would you! —
Fer he had riz an' faced around,
    An' stood there, smilin', as they brung
The turkey in, all stuffed an' browned —

Too sweet fer nose er tooth er tongue!
  With sniffs o' sage, an' p'raps a dash
Of old burnt brandy, steamin' hot
  Mixed kind o' in with apple-mash,
An' mince-meat, an' the Lord knows what!
Nobody was a-talkin' then
  To 'filliate my awk'ardness —
  No noise o' any kind, but jes'
The rattle o' the dishes when
They'd fetch 'em in an' set 'em down,
An' fix an' change 'em round an' round,
  Like women does — Till mother says, —
  "Vittels is ready; Abner, call
  Down S'repty — she's up stairs, I guess." —
And Marg'et *she* says, "Ef you bawl
Like that, she'll not come down at all!
Besides, we needn't wait till she
Gits down! Here, Tomps, set down by me,
  An' Pap, say grace!" Well, there I was,
What *could* I do! I drapped my head
Behind my fists an' groaned, an' said: —
  "Indulgent Parent! in Thy cause
  We bow the head an' bend the knee,

An' break the bread, an' pour the wine,
    Feelin'"— (The stair-door suddenly
    Went bang! an' S'repty flounced by me)—
"Feelin'," I says, "this feast is Thine—
    This New Year's feast"—An' rap-rap-rap!
    Went Marg'et's case-knife on her plate—
    An' next, I heerd a sasser drap,—
    Then I looked up, an' strange to state,
There S'repty set in Tomps's lap—
    An' huggin' him, as shore as fate!—
An' mother kissin' him k-slap!
An' Marg'et — she chips in to drap
    The ruther peert remark to me:—
"That 'grace' o' yourn," she says, "wont
        'gee'—
    This haint no '*New Year's feast,*'" says she,—
"*This is a' Infair Dinner, Pap!*"

An' so it was!—Ben married fer
    Purt'nigh a week!—'Twas Marg'et planned
    The whole thing fer 'em, through an'
        through.
    I'm reconciled; an', understand,

I take things jes' as they occur,—
    Ef *Marg'et* liked Tomps, Tomps 'ud do!
But I-says-I, a-holt his hand,—
"I'm glad you didn't marry HER—
    'Cause Marg'et's *my guardeen*—Yes, *sir!*—
    An' S'repty's good enough fer you!"

THE TOWN KARNTEEL.

THE town Karnteel!—It's who'll reveal
    Its praises jushtifiable?
For who can sing av anything
    So lovely and reliable?
Whin Summer, Spring, or Winter lies
    From Malin's Head to Tipperary,
There's no such town for interprise
    Bechuxt Youghal and Londonderry!

There's not its likes in Ireland—
    For twic't the week, be-gorries!
They're playing jigs upon the band—
And joomping there in sacks—and—and—
    And racing, wid wheel-borries!

Karnteel—its there, like any fair,
    The purty gurrls is plinty, sure!—
And, man-alive! at forty-five
    The legs av me air twinty, sure!

I lave me cares, and hoein', too,
  Behint me, as is sinsible,
And its Karnteel I'm goin' to,
  To cilebrate in principal!

For there's the town av all the land!
  And twic't the week, be-gorries!
They're playing jigs upon the band,
And joomping there in sacks — and — and —
  And racing, wid wheel-borries!

And whilst I feel for ould Karnteel
  That I've no phrases glorious,
It stands above the need av love
  That boasts in voice uproarious! —
Lave that for Cork, and Dublin, too,
  And Armagh and Killarney, thin, —
And Karnteel won't be troublin' you
  Wid any jilous blarney, thin!

For there's the town av all the land,
  Where twic't the week, be-gorries!
They're playing jigs upon the band —
And joomping there in sacks — and —and —
  And racing, wid wheel-borries!

SENCE I tuck holt o' Gibbses Churn
 And ben a-handlin' the concern,
I've traveled round the grand ole State
Of Indiany lots, of late!
I've canvassed Crawferdsville and sweat
Around the town of Lafayette;
I've saw a many a County-seat
I ust to think was hard to beat:
At constant dreenage and expense
I've worked Greencastle and Vincennes —
Drapped out o' Putnam into Clay,
Owen, and on down thataway
Plum' into Knox, on the back-track
Fer home agin — and glad I'm back! —
I've saw these towns, as I say — but
They's none 'at beats ole Terry Hut!

Its more'n likely you'll insist
I claim this 'cause I'm predjudist,

Bein' born'd here in ole Vygo
In sight o' Terry Hut; — but no,
Yer clean dead wrong! — and I maintain
They's nary drap in ary vein
O' mine but what's as free as air
To jest take issue with you there! —
'Cause, boy and man, fer forty year,
I've argied *aginst* livin' here,
And jawed around and traded lies
About our lack o' enterprise;
And tuck and turned in and agreed
All other towns was in the lead,
When — drat my melts! — they couldn't cut
No shine a-tall with Terry Hut!

Take, even, statesmanship and wit,
And ginerel git-up-and-git, —
Ole Terry Hut is sound clean through! —
Turn ole Dick Thompson loose, er Dan
Vorehees — and where's they any man
Kin even hold a candle to
Their eloquence? And where's as clean
A fi-nan-seer as Rile' McKeen —
Er puorer, in his daily walk,

In railroad er in racin' stock!
And there's 'Gene Debs — a man 'at stands
And jest holds out in his two hands
As warm a heart as ever beat
Betwixt here and the Jedgement Seat!—
All these is reasons why I put
Sich bulk o' faith in Terry Hut.

So I've come back, with eyes 'at sees
My faults, at last,— to make my peace
With this old place, and truthful swear —
Like Gineral Tom Nelson does,—
"They haint no city anywhere
On God's green earth lays over us!"
Our city govament is *grand* —
"Ner is they better farmin'-land
Sun-kissed"—as Tom goes on and says—
"Er dower'd with sich advantages!"
And I've come back, with welcome tread,
From journeyin's vain, as I have said,
To settle down in ca'm content,
And cuss the towns where I have went,
And brag on ourn and boast and strut
Around the streets o' Terry Hut!

LEEDLE DUTCH BABY.

LEEDLE Dutch baby haff come ter town!
  Jabber und jump till der day gone down —
Jabber und sphlutter, und sphlit hees jaws —
Vot a Dutch baby dees Launsmon vas!
I dink dose mout' vas leedle too vide
Ober he laugh fon dot also-side!
Haff got blenty off deemple und vrown —
Hey! leedle Dutchman, come ter town!

Leedle Dutch baby, I dink me proud
Ober your fader can schquall dot loud
Ven he vas leedle Dutch baby like you,
Und yoost don't gare like he alvays do! —
Guess ven dey vean him on beer, you bet
Dot's der because dot he aind veaned yet! —
Vot you said off he drink you down?
Hey! leedle Dutchman, come ter town!

Leedle Dutch baby, yoost schquall avay—
Schquall fon preakfast till gisterday!
Better you all time cry und shout
Dan shmile me vonce fon der coffin out!
Vot I gare off you keek my nose
Downside-up mit your heels unt toes—
Downside, oder der upside-down.—
Hey! leedle Dutchman, come ter town!

DOWN ON WRIGGLE CRICK.

Best Time to Kill a Hog 's when He 's Fat.—Old Saw.

MOSTLY, folks is law abidin',
    Down on Wriggle Crick,—
Seein' they's no 'Squire residin'
    In our bailywick;
No grand-juries—no suppeenies,
    Ner no vested rights to pick
Out yer man, jerk up and jail ef
    He's outragin' Wriggle Crick!

Wriggle Crick haint got no lawin',
    Ner no suits to beat;
Ner no court-house gee-and-hawin'
    Like a county-seat;
Haint no waitin' round fer verdicks,
    Ner non-gittin' witness-fees:
Ner no thiefs 'at gits "new hearin's,"
    By some lawyer slick as grease!

Wriggle Cricks's leadin' spirit
　　Is old Johnts Culwell,—
Keeps postoffice, and right near it
　　Owns what's called "The Grand Hotel"—
(Warehouse now)—buys wheat and ships it;
　　Gits out ties, and trades in stock,
And knows all the high-toned drummers
　　'Twixt South Bend and Mishawauk.

Last year comes along a feller—
　　Sharper 'an a lance,—
Stovepipe-hat, and silk umbreller,
　　And a boughten all-wool pants,—
Tinkerin' of clocks and watches;
　　Says a trial's all he wants—
And rents out the tavern-office
　　Next to uncle Johnts.

Well.—He tacked up his k'dentials,
　　And got down to biz.—
Captured Johnts by cuttin' stencils
　　Fer them old wheat-sacks o' his.—

Fixed his clock, in the postoffice —
    Painted fer him, clean and slick,
'Crost his safe in gold-leaf letters,
    "J. Cullwells's, Wriggle Crick."

Any kind o' job you keered to
    Resk him with, and bring,
He'd fix fer you — jest appeared to
    Turn his hand to anything! —
Rings, er earbobs, er umbrellers —
    Glue a cheer, er chany doll, —
W'y, of all the beatin' fellers
    He jest beat 'em all!

Made his friends, but wouldn't stop there, —
    One mistake he learnt,
That was, sleepin' in his shop there. —
    And one Sunday night it burnt!
Come in one o' jest a-sweepin'
    All the whole town high and dry —
And that feller, when they waked him,
    Suffocatin', mighty nigh!

Johnts he drug him from the buildin',
  Helpless — 'peared to be, —
And the women and the childern
  Drenchin' him with sympathy!
But I noticed Johnts helt on him
  With a' extry lovin' grip,
And the men-folks gethered round him
  In most warmest pardership!

That's the whole mess, grease and dopin'!
  Johnts's safe was saved, —
But the lock was found sprung open,
  And the inside caved.
Was no trial — ner no jury —
  Ner no jedge ner court-house-click, —
Circumstances alters cases
  Down on Wriggle Crick!

WHEN DE FOLKS IS GONE.

WHAT dat scratchin' at de kitchin' do'?
 Done heah'n dat foh an hour er mo'!
Tell you, Mr. Niggah, das sho's yo' bo'n,
Hit's might lonesome waitin' when de folks is
  gone!

Blame my trap! how de wind do blow!
An' dis is das' de night foh de witches, sho'!
Dey's trouble gon' to waste when de ole slut
  whine,
An' you heah de cat a-spittin' when de moon don't
  shine!

Chune my fiddle, an' de bridge go "*bang!*"
An' I lef 'er right back whah she allus hang,
An' de tribble snap short an' de apern split
When dey no mortal man wah a-techin' hit!

Dah! *Now,* what! How de ole j'ice cracks!
'Spec' dis house, ef hit tell plain fac's,
'Ud talk about de ha'nts wid dey long tails on
What das'n't on'y come when de folks is gone!

What I tuk an' done ef a sho'-nuff ghos'
Pop right up by de ole bed-pos'?
What dat shinin' fru de front do' crack? . . . .
God bress de Lo'd! hit's de folks got back!

THE LITTLE TOWN O' TAILHOLT.

YOU kin boast about yer cities, and their stiddy
    growth and size,
And brag about yer county-seats, and business
    enterprise,
And railroads, and factories, and all sich foolery—
But the little Town o' Tailholt is big enough fer
    me!

You can harp about yer churches, with their
    steeples in the clouds,
And gas about yer graded streets, and blow about
    yer crowds;
You kin talk about yer theaters, and all you've
    got to see —
But the little Town o' Tailholt is show enough fer
    me!

They haint no style in our town — hit's little-like
    and small —
They haint no *churches*, nuther,— jes' the meetin'-
    house is all;

They's no sidewalks, to speak of — but the
        highway's allus free,
And the little Town o' Tailholt is wide enough fer
        me!

Some finds its discommodin'-like, I'm willin' to
        admit,
To hev but one postoffice, and a womern keepin'
        hit,
And the drugstore, and shoeshop, and grocery, all
        three —
But the little Town o' Tailholt is handy 'nough
        fer me!

You kin smile, and turn yer nose up, and joke
        and hev yer fun,
And laugh and holler "Tail-holts is better holts 'n
        none!"
Ef the city suits you better, w'y, hits where
        you'd orto' be,
But the little Town o' Tailholt 's good enough fer
        me!